BRITAIN IN OLD PHOTOGRAPHS

HASTINGS &
ST LEONARDS-ON-SEA

GAVIN HAINES

SUTTON PUBLISHING LIMITED

Sutton Publishing Limited
Phoenix Mill · Thrupp · Stroud
Gloucestershire · GL5 2BU

First published 199

Copyright © Gavin Haines, 1997

Cover photographs, front: looking east from the
foreshore near the harbour arm; *back*: corner of
Devonshire Road, 1901 (see p. 53). *Page 1*:
castle, looking west, 1904, with three ladies
seated.

British Library Cataloguing in Publication Data
A catalogue record for this book is available from the
British Library.

ISBN 0-7509-1355-X

Typeset in 10/12 Perpetua.
Typesetting and origination by
Sutton Publishing Limited.
Printed in Great Britain by
Ebenezer Baylis, Worcester.

Luggers, looking west from beach, 1901. Before the invention of nylon, nets had to be laid out in the sun to dry, or they would rot. One of these traditional luggers, called the *Enterprise*, has been preserved in the fisherman's museum. Mr Lazarus is the man in the foreground.

CONTENTS

Cambridge Gardens, looking east, 1917. These First World War soldiers are billeted with a Hastings landlady at No. 23 Cambridge Gardens. The sign above the door tells us that she still has a bedroom to let.

INTRODUCTION

A photograph is a view of the world at an instant of time. Architectural styles, fashions, and means of transport change with the times, and the photographs in this book will show this change. From the fire on the pier to the destruction of The Memorial and the last days of steam trains at Hastings station, old photographs are a wonderful source of history. Whatever your interest, let this book inspire you to get out and use your camera. It does not matter whether you are an amateur or professional – the principles and techniques of photography are the same for everyone.

Why not follow in the footsteps of the photographers of old? Can you take a photograph from where the tripod stood all those years ago? You may follow the route that the book takes on foot, but some of the viewpoints are no longer accessible.

A short walk along the seafront and through the town centre will take you past most of the viewpoints featured in this book. A more demanding walk over the East and West Hills will take you to the spectacular viewpoints so delighted in by Victorian and Edwardian photographers.

If there is little in the scene to indicate the date, no people, cars, or buses, a photograph could be very old, possibly 1870 or earlier. Old photographs were taken using different processes to modern photography: they used a larger format and a different chemical process. You can often tell the age of a photograph by the type of camera and process used. However, the fact that a photograph is sepia toned, blurred or very faded does not necessarily mean that it is very old. The techniques used in early photography can produce results which are superior to modern photography. A sharp black and white photograph could have been taken fifty years before a faded sepia print.

Long exposure times meant that early photography was limited to empty streets and formal poses – anything which moved as the photograph was taken would come out as a blur. Early photographs of the town used the wet collodion process, invented in 1851. Although collodion (a kind of jelly) is a technically demanding process, failures are few and the emulsion is fast enough for snapshots in a good light. Dry plates were invented in 1871, and were available commercially by 1874, so any pictures taken of the town on glass plates must be after this date. The first simple method of photography which anybody could use was the Kodak roll film camera introduced in 1888. The first camera to use 35mm film, called the Leica, was manufactured in 1924 by Leitz.

Photographers began working in Hastings almost as soon as photography was invented – the very first newspaper advertisement appeared in the *Hastings and St Leonards News* on 19 April 1850. It read: 'PORTRAITS TAKEN IN A FEW SECONDS'. There was such a demand that by February 1851 the photographer, Mr Beaufort, was taking over a hundred Daguerreotype portraits a week. By 1854 many professional men had entered the lucrative photography business, including Thomas Mann, whose collodion prints of streets taken around The Memorial 120 years or more ago appear in this book.

Queen Victoria's husband, Prince Albert, died on 14 December 1861 and a meeting of subscribers decided to build a memorial to him in the form of a Gothic clock tower on 10 March 1862. The Memorial was completed when the clock arrived on 10 June 1864. The earliest photograph of The Memorial so far published shows it without the clock, but there is an earlier picture in this book. The clock tower was demolished in the 1970s, but the place where it stood has continued to be known to local people as 'The Memorial'.

Some of the photographs in this book have been made directly from the original glass plate or negative film; others are from existing prints. The photographers of old often did their own developing, and made additional prints of subjects they liked: other collectors may well have copies of photographs which you believe to be unique. However, all the railway pictures in this book were taken by John Powys when he was at the Grammar School. He developed the film himself and I have made the prints, so they are truly unique and have never before been published.

The seaside has always been a popular destination and from the eighteenth century, accommodation for visitors gradually extended along from the Old Town. Most of the present town centre was built in the nineteenth century. Carlisle Parade was built in 1850 and embellished with a lion and a unicorn from Buckingham Palace in 1854. (The architect, A.J. Humbert, was also employed by Prince Albert.) The first train arrived at the station in 1851 and with it Hastings's heyday.

But the cheerful and crowded holiday town featured in these old photographs later met with disaster. . . .

On 26 July 1940 a lone fighter-bomber circled the town, unloading eleven high explosives. Several houses were demolished. Attacks on a much bigger scale were to follow. On the following day a formation of fifty planes flew up the Channel and attacked St Leonards. There were numerous attacks after that, and many lives were lost as homes, hotels and boarding houses were destroyed.

If you are not able to identify the places in the old photographs, this is the reason: the town had little aerial defence, and enemy planes often circled round, machine gunning and dropping bombs as they liked. There were anti-aircraft guns situated around the town, and heavy guns on the West Hill as a defence against flying bombs (V1s), but the scale of the attack often made effective defence impossible. So the photographs are of Hastings but the buildings have been demolished and their sites re-built. You can work out where a place is by taking the book along, and identifying landmarks like the castle in the background.

By the end of the war the Nazis had dropped a total of 550 high explosive bombs and 750 incendiaries on the town. Towards the end of the war an additional sixteen flying bombs or 'doodlebugs' crashed into the town. A total of 463 properties were destroyed, 14,818 properties were damaged, 154 people were killed, 260 were seriously injured and 439 were slightly injured. It took the town many years to recover. In 1921 the population had been 67,494. It had gone down to 48,820 by 1945 as a result of the war. By 1961 it had crept up to 66,428, but this was only a few more than the figure for 1901 (65,528). At the last census (1991) the figure stood at 80,820.

Since these eventful days the town has continued to witness many changes. Hemlines have risen and fallen, well-loved and remembered landmarks and shops have disappeared to be replaced by new ones, and cars which once circled the memorial clock now wait at traffic lights to cross the pedestrian area. Browse through these pages and remember, but also look forward to changes yet to come.

THE OLD TOWN

Teas at Lift, Old Town, looking west from the East Hill, 1926. If you walked up instead of taking the lift, you deserved a ginger beer. The lady's accessories have complementary polka dots. St Leonards Pier in the background enables us to date this photograph to before the Second World War when the pier was wrecked.

All Saints' Church, looking west from the East Hill, 1868. The church is seen before restoration to the designs of Mr Butterfield in 1870. The steam mill on the West Hill on the right of the picture was built in 1849 by Mr Ward of Ore, and demolished in 1874.

East Hill Lift, 1930. You might consider the lift to be a funicular railway. It is the steepest in the country – with an angle of 38 degrees. The tank underneath the car coming down has been filled with water, which is then emptied at the bottom and pumped back up to the top.

Tackleway, looking west from the East Hill, 1906. You can take a ride in the lift to reach this vantage point. The girl is holding her hat, so it is a typically windy day in Hastings. The man in the uniform belongs to the East Hill Lift, which opened on 9 April 1902. The new harbour arm is under construction, on the left of the picture.

Tackleway, looking west from the East Hill, 1930. Compare this with the earlier view from the East Hill, and you can see that a considerable volume of shingle has accumulated behind the harbour arm. This picture shows Hastings Pier, modernised in 1928, with an excursion paddle steamer setting off eastwards.

A natural ice. Old Town boys enjoy playing with the ice frozen in a horse trough in The Bourne, 1925. The boy in the middle appears to be sucking the ice, which might not have been savoury if the horse had been along recently. . . .

Mending nets, 1901. The fishermen in this picture are wearing bowler hats; this was popular hard hat headgear.

Brewery, 1865. This is a very early print of the Brewery in The Bourne, which is in the Old Town.

Bourne Street and a postman, looking south, 1900. The house in the centre survives from the late fifteenth century. It originally faced on to a square, later occupied by the brick warehouse on the right. The postman is standing in the middle of what is now the busy A259 through road.

Fishermen's Beach, 'The Stade', looking west, 1930. The fishing boats now have propellers, but are still equipped for sail. Hastings had the largest fishing fleet worked from a beach.

Fishermen's Beach, 'The Stade', looking north, 1950. A cross-section of small British family cars – Ford, Morris and Austin – have been driven down for the day. This is a difficult picture to date, but it must have been taken just after the war, as there are two pill boxes on the East Hill. The Stade, which is also the fishermen's working beach, is very tidy.

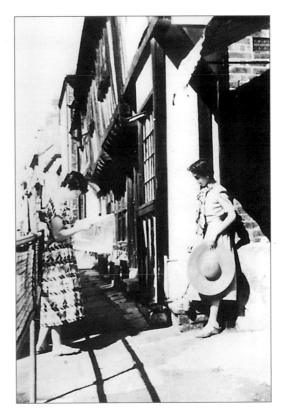

All Saints' Street, looking north, 1960. Some of the oldest surviving houses dating from 1450 are in this street. Much of the medieval Old Town would have looked like this, although the timber framing would have been a lighter colour.

Children paddling by the harbour arm, looking east from the beach, 1898. The bucket and spade brigade are engaging in a traditional seaside pastime. Note the costumes worn for this activity.

Boating lake, looking east, 1964. The miniature railway was constructed in June 1948 and operated with scaled-down steam engines. These were subsequently replaced by diesel locomotives which do not need water.

Boating lake, looking west, 1962. Houses in Marine Parade (to the left of the Royal Albion), which were destroyed by a gas explosion on 13 July 1963. Thirty people were injured, but nobody was killed. The houses were never re-built.

Reflections in the boating lake, looking north, 1960. East Parade was the first attempt to provide a fashionable walk by the sea for visitors in the late eighteenth century. On a winter's day, November 1960, we see the houses beautifully reflected in the boating lake.

Lifeboat house, looking east, 1895. The building in the background which looks like an aircraft hangar was used for concerts featuring minstrels with banjos. The lifeboat house was built in 1882 and demolished in 1959.

East Parade from the beach, looking north, 1901. The remains of the Elizabethan harbour seen in this picture are now under the boating lake. The interesting buildings behind include the Cutter, the Lower Light (next to the Rising Sun), the Victorian lifeboat house (with turret), and on the right the Rotunda (circular) fish market.

The Rising Sun, looking north, 1900. This is an enlargement of the view above. The Rising Sun, a good name for a pub facing the sea, was built before 1854.

Marine Parade, looking north, 1900. The Cutter was built in 1792. During the exciting times of the Napoleonic Wars the landlord was James Bell, from 1807 to 1823. He had been a former valet to Lord Nelson. The façade has since been considerably altered.

Lifeboat house, looking east, 1900. The old Victorian lifeboat house was demolished on 5 December 1959. The 'shaving' sign appears to be falling down in another view, but this picture shows it was at an angle.

Boating lake, looking west, 1965. Grappling hooks are being used. After the Second World War the boating lake became very popular once again. The motor boats had little Stuart-Turner engines. They were eventually sold off as collectors' items.

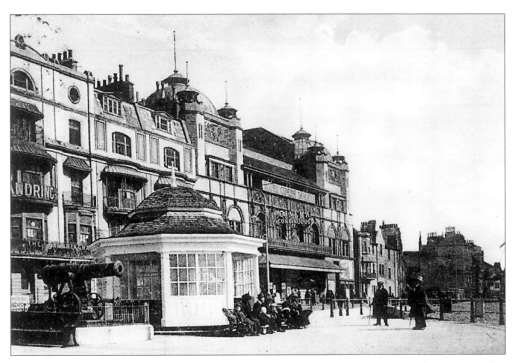

De Luxe Cinema and the Russian gun, looking east, 1910. The cinema is decorated with terracotta tiles, which has made restoration a difficult problem. It is now a bingo hall and amusement arcade.

Beach Terrace, looking west, 1900. This terrace was in front of Pelham Crescent. Residents were always agitating to have these old lodging houses pulled down as they spoiled the view. The Russian gun was sent to Hastings from the Admiralty as a British trophy of the Crimean War on 9 October 1857. It was contributed as scrap metal to help the war effort on 4 April 1942.

High Street, looking north, 1937. The car is a 14 hp Armstrong-Siddeley, dating from 1937. The well-to-do lady is surely the owner of the car, which must have travelled on the continent since it has a GB plate on the back. The little cottage has been dated to the seventeenth century.

TOWN CENTRE

The Memorial, looking east from Cambridge Road, 1956. The Leyland TD5 was one of the last open-topped buses to be built as such in 1939, but owing to the war they never fulfilled their original purpose. Later open-top buses are just ordinary double-deckers which have been converted.

Shell sellers on the seafront, near Harold Place, 1900. This picture reminds us of that tongue-twister 'She sells sea shells beside the sea shore.' She wears a flower-trimmed straw hat, a fur-trimmed pelisse and a silk apron.

Looking north at Denmark Place from the foreshore, 1919. An empty German submarine U118 was washed ashore on 19 April 1919 in front of Harold Place, after breaking its tow rope on the way from Cherbourg to Scapa Flow. It was welcomed as an unusual Easter attraction, until a build-up of chlorine gas poisoned a group of coastguards, one of whom died on 21 February 1920.

Denmark Place, looking east, 1948. The Carlisle Saloon was originally the Pelham Hotel in 1892. Bomb damage to Caroline Place reveals that this is a post-Second World War picture.

Carlisle Parade, looking west, 1933. The underground car park was an imaginative development in the 1930s when nobody could foresee the present volume of traffic. The ventilation towers, which have fans to remove the fumes, are disguised as two matching public shelters.

Queen's Hotel, looking north, 1895. Only one of the two cupolas on the roof of the hotel is visible: it was a place to which smokers were banished. The original sea wall visible in this photo is now inside the underground car park.

Queen's Hotel and pleasure yachts, looking west, 1895. This is a similar view to the photo above, from a slightly different perspective.

Queen's Hotel, looking north, 1906. A Social Democratic Federation (SDF) meeting is being held on the beach. The Council had passed a byelaw against political meetings which did not apply if you held the meeting on the beach. Robert Tressell, author of *The Ragged Trousered Philanthropists*, is in the picture. The little girl by the SDF banner is Kathleen Noonan, his daughter.

Queen's Hotel, looking west, 1910. This shows the forecourt of the hotel before the seafront was widened. In the foreground is the big capstan for winching up the pleasure yachts.

The Memorial, looking west, 1890. There is much to be looked at in this picture including horse buses, trade carts and cyclists.

Reeves Corner, looking west, 1890. This is on the site of the bridge over the Priory Stream. The buildings on the right were replaced by the National Westminster Bank in 1924. The wonderful cart is delivering goods.

Bewlay's, looking north from Robertson Street, 1960. This tobacconist's stood on the corner of Cambridge Road and Robertson Street for many years. In Hastings there seem to be never-ending roadworks.

Bodega Bars, looking north from Robertson Street, 1960. This corner building was originally the music hall where Charles Dickens gave a reading from *The Pickwick Papers* and *A Christmas Carol* in 1861. There were two lines of waiting carriages stretching for half a mile up Cambridge Road. It was later converted into a cinema, and then a shop.

Brassey Institute, looking east from Trinity Street, 1977. This is a literary corner, showing Howes bookshop and the public library. The Brassey Institute is an example of decorative Venetian Gothic architecture, designed by Mr Vernon. The figure on the bike is Robert Meredith, an erstwhile library assistant.

The Memorial topping out, looking north from Harold Place, 1863. Prince Albert died on 14 December 1861, and on 10 March 1862 a meeting of subscribers decided to build The Memorial. Prince Albert's statue arrived from Liverpool on 3 July 1863, and this photo shows the 'topping out' ceremony. The clock arrived from Messrs Thwaites & Reed, Clerkenwell, on 10 June 1864.

The Memorial at 9.40 a.m., looking east, 1870. Visitors complained about the dirty state of roads near The Memorial, and suggested that able-bodied paupers should sweep crossings. They were also annoyed by the coarse remarks and bad language used by loungers at the corners of streets in the neighbourhood.

The Memorial at 3.15 p.m., looking east, 1900. Shop blinds have been lowered to protect the goods from the summer sun. The York, to the left, was a famous Victorian pub, much frequented at elections. The wide-angle lens used to take this picture creates a false perspective which enables us to see round the corner of Pelham Street.

Trams in Robertson Street, looking east, 1910. This tram is going to Bexhill, but overhead wires were not allowed on the seafront so the very early trams (before 1914) used the Dolter stud-contact system, which sometimes electrocuted horses. The surface of the street is made from wood blocks.

The Memorial, looking east from Cambridge Road, 1928. One of the first trolley buses, built by Guy Motors, can be seen. Electrical equipment was supplied by the British Thomson-Houston Company. Each bus had two 40 hp self-ventilated interpole traction motors, consuming 500 volts at 70 amps.

The Memorial at 3.20 p.m., looking east, 1929. The post office moved to Cambridge Road in 1930, and the tram lines were gone by 1929, so this picture can be accurately dated. Wards, the outfitters, was to open on the site of the old post office (on the extreme left of the picture) in 1933.

'Adam's washing' flutters around The Memorial, looking north from Harold Place, 1960. The white car in the centre is a Morris Oxford, a Ford Popular is on the left and the car on the right is an Austin. The bunting (flags) was known locally as 'Adam's washing'.

Snow at The Memorial, looking north from Harold Place, 1962. The winter of December and January 1962/3 was very severe, and absolutely everything froze, including the sea. We see intrepid shoppers making their way through the snow, and possibly ending up at the RESH (Royal East Sussex Hospital). It does look cold!

Clearing the snow with bulldozer, looking west to Cambridge Road, 1962. In the background is the old-established toy shop Jepsons, which originally started at 72 Norman Road – now sadly no more. The bulldozer and the truck are of historical interest. The snow was taken to Rock-a-Nore and the huge pile did not melt until June.

The Memorial, looking north from Harold Place, 1962.

Picture seller at The Memorial, looking east, 1981. Although the clock tower has gone, this part of Hastings is still known as The Memorial. Here a picture seller adds liveliness to the scene.

QUEEN'S ROAD & ALEXANDRA PARK

Queen's Road, looking north, 1955. The trolley bus is one of the models made by AEC (Associated Equipment Co.) of Southall, Middlesex, delivered in 1940. The car nearest the camera is a Standard. Ward's new building was opened on the old post office site in 1933.

The entrance to the former coach station, looking west, 1990. The flower seller is Polly O'Keefe, who was born in Barnsley, West Yorkshire. She used to work at the Royal East Sussex Hospital as a nursing auxiliary on Ward 5. She says: 'You do see life, selling flowers – mostly sad times. It was a happy day when the Queen came to open the Shopping Centre. Councillor Pam Brown looked so nice, I took no notice of the Queen!'

Queen's Parade before demolition, looking south, 1990. This sad row of shops is under sentence of death, but there has been a stay of execution while the financial details of the development are sorted out. This is now the east side of the Priory Meadow Shopping Centre.

Priory Meadow and the old station, looking west, 1860. Priory Meadow was first suggested as a cricket ground in 1863; it was levelled and drained in April 1864. The ditch was filled up and the stream diverted at a cost of £500. The tenants of Priory Farm received notice to quit so that the land could be sold for building in 1865. The line going up the hill is the sandstone boundary wall of Summerfields at Brisco's Walk. This estate has now become the Civic Centre.

Cricket ground, looking west from the Ladies' Parlour, 1927. This interesting view shows the layout of the Victorian station before reconstruction in 1931. Compare with the 1860 picture above.

Princess Elizabeth and the Mayor, 12 May 1951. A great crowd has assembled at the cricket ground to see the then Princess Elizabeth receive the deeds of the castle and hand them to the Mayor, Alderman Arthur Chambers, for safe keeping. A union flag hangs from Marks and Spencer in the background.

Corner of Queen's Road and South Terrace, 1950. This corner was popular with followers of cricket since it was possible to watch the game from here without having to pay.

Cricket ground, looking east, 1989. Followers of cricket laze in the sun, as the last county match at the ground is played out.

The last cricket match, looking north, 1989. In this eventide picture we see the rays of the sun slanting down on the last county game to be played at the ground before the development; and worse still, as the shadows grew longer, Sussex lost to Kent. The original Victorian pavilion can be seen in the background.

Statues at Park Gates, looking west from St Andrew's Bridge, 1920. The two Norman knights in the garden of this house at the Park Gates are very imposing. They have unfortunately now disappeared. The house, called Saxonhurst, was built by Joseph Catt in 1870.

Entrance to the park with flower beds, looking west from the top of Queen's Road, 1939. The war memorial was unveiled by the Earl of Cavan, the Royal Sussex Regiment and ex-service men led by Col. F.G. Langham on 26 March 1922. Alderman W.J. Fellows JP was mayor and treasurer of the war memorial fund.

Boating lake, 1900. Alexandra Park was originally opened as St Andrew's Pleasure Grounds. Dogs became a major nuisance, and the subject of police surveillance. Dogs without collars would be taken and destroyed if not claimed within twenty-four hours.

Boating in the park, 1900. The schoolboys are wearing caps and their girlfriends have straw boaters. The rowers in this relaxing scene could have no idea of the century of death and destruction which was soon to follow.

The old gas showroom and St Andrew's Church, 1970. The church was consecrated by the Bishop of Chichester on 30 November 1870. A panel of the mural by Robert Tressell was saved by David Haines during the demolition on 29 August 1970. The church was very dangerous and those trying to save the mural were threatened with eviction for being uninsured. The last stage of demolition was on 5 September 1970.

St Andrew's Church, 1970. The church had been vandalised with obscene French slogans in 1966. The person who did it, known locally as 'The Dauber', was never caught. Fred Ball and his daughter, Clare, are with David Haines, who is cleaning part of the Robert Tressell mural which had been whitewashed over.

Interior of St Andrew's Church, 1950. Robert Tressell painted this superb mural in 1904; he worked during the night to avoid interruptions. The panel on the extreme left of the picture (now displayed in the Old Town Museum) was the only part of the mural which could be saved. It was later restored following an appeal.

Outside the old Labour Party House at 25 Wellington Square, 1973. Neil Kinnock, who subsequently became leader of the Labour Party, is holding a copy of *One of the Damned*, Fred Ball's biography of Robert Tressell.

Fred Ball and Kathleen Noonan-Lynne, 13 December 1968. Kathleen, daughter of Robert Tressell, was invited to Hastings by the local Trades Council, and their union banners are in the background. She was presented with a television set which can just be seen on the left. Fred Ball was a local author who was instrumental in saving the complete manuscript of *The Ragged Trousered Philanthropists*.

The circus comes to town, 1892! This photograph was taken in Queen's Road at the junction with South Terrace. The box containing the plates from which these pictures were made is inscribed 'Sanger's Circus'. This circus, owned by Lord John Sanger and Sons, performed at the Central Cricket Ground on 15 and 16 August 1892. On the left is the Cricketers' Pub, a favourite haunt of Robert Tressell.

Circus parade, looking north, 1892. Fascinated spectators in a wonderful variety of hats admire splendidly dressed riders.

Queen's Road, looking north, 1892. This man, sporting a fez, is on his way to perform with his elephant at the cricket ground.

Circus parade, looking north, 1892. Circus horses with their gaily dressed riders are coming down Queen's Road. The man on the ladder has stopped his work to watch the spectacle.

Circus parade, 1892. The men on their wagons have a good vantage point to watch the circus parade. St Andrew's Square can be seen in the background.

Circus parade, looking north, 1892. People line the street to watch. Note how everyone, even the children, wears hats. A child in a splendid frilled bonnet is lifted on to her father's shoulder to see above the crowd.

Queen's Road, looking north, 1892. The dog on the left is totally uninterested in the parade of Indian elephants coming down Queen's Road. The elephant keepers in their uniforms march along beside their animals.

An enlargement of the photograph on the back cover, giving a closer view of the Central Cricket Ground and Queen's Road from the junction of Devonshire Road with South Terrace, 1901. The awnings over the old shops in Queen's Road can be seen. The shop on the corner was destined to become Marks and Spencer. It was called J. Hepworth and Sons and sold refreshments. A note left with the glass plate gives us the date – 25 July 1901.

Cricket ground, looking east, 1960. The row of shops which comprised Queen's Parade have yet to be built, but once this happened, the final fate of the cricket ground was sealed forever.

St Andrew's Arch, looking north, 1896. A survey in 1866 reported that 'the arch over Ore Lane has become dangerous as it has sunk considerably'. There was talk of a new iron girder bridge. The locomotive is unfortunately just out of the picture, but most of this Ore to Hastings train is clearly shown. The houses in St Helen's Road are visible through the tunnel.

St Andrew's Arch during demolition, looking south, 1896. These are the final moments of St Andrew's Arch.

St Andrew's Bridge newly constructed, looking south, 1899. The road has now been widened, but this is a view which has otherwise remained much the same.

St Andrew's Bridge, looking west, 1957. The absence of vegetation dates this picture to the days when the railway had plenty of staff: the embankment is kept cropped. The engine is for you to identify.

The park, looking south, 1901. This shows volunteers for the South African war practising by building a pontoon bridge on the boating lake in Alexandra Park.

The park, looking east, 1901. Volunteers float the pontoon into place.

Volunteers proceeding to Aldershot, Station Approach, 1901. This photo is also particularly interesting as it gives us a rare glimpse of Hastings station before the 1931 reconstruction. I have included this and other photos to inspire railway modellers to complete a Victorian-era project.

Volunteers with bicycles, looking east, 1901. A young boy watches, perhaps wishing he were old enough to wear the uniform. Within a few years he might have been in the trenches, perhaps on the Somme.

Huffey's Corner with *Evening News* van, looking west, 1960. The authorities wanted to get rid of the newspaper shop when Station Approach was re-modelled in 1931, but Mr Huffey, the newsagent, hung on to this lucrative corner site. The shop was finally forced to move to Havelock Road in 1996 when the Priory Meadow Shopping Centre was built. The *Evening News* vehicle is an A35 van.

Hastings station in British Rail days, 1967. The station still has the old pre-nationalisation facia. The car on the extreme right is a Triumph Herald, while that in front of the entrance is a Vauxhall and the one next to it is a Ford Cortina. The miniskirt also dates this picture to the 1960s.

TWILIGHT OF STEAM

Locomotive No. 33033 Q1 leaving the goods yard, looking west from Earl Street Bridge, 1957. The entrance to Hastings station is just visible in the top right-hand corner of this picture. This was almost a contra-jour shot taken by the evening light, which dramatises the pathos of the scene. Poor old British Rail locomotives suffered terribly at the end – hissing steam and leaking oil.

Locomotive No. 32338 at platform 1, 1957. This is Billington's (London Brighton & South Coast Railway) 2–6–0 express goods engine, class K, built in 1913 at Brighton. There were originally seventeen, but none have been preserved. They were originally built to haul continental goods traffic on the Newhaven–Dieppe route before the First World War, but lived to see the end of steam as this picture shows.

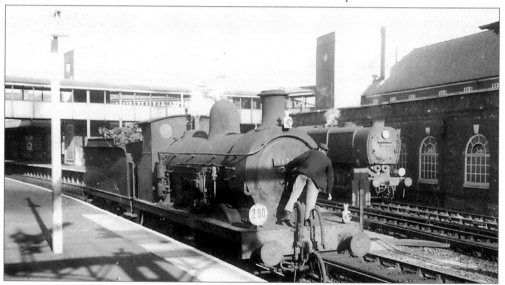

Locomotive 3171XX, looking east, 1957. This eventide picture shows a Wainwright South Eastern & Chatham Railway standard goods class C 0–6–0 on platform 1. In total 109 of these locomotives were built at Ashford from 1900 to 1908. Only one has been preserved (No. 31592), on the Bluebell Railway.

Locomotive No. 32338 with driver, looking west, 1957. This is a closer view of the class K 338 engine in the previous picture. Details of the cab are clearly visible.

Excursion train, Cornwallis Bridge, 1957. The LBSC K class 2–6–0 No. 32338, built in 1913 at Brighton Works, is pulling standard SR corridor stock. The loco and carriages are too wide for the Mountfield Tunnel, so it must be an excursion along the coast and not a Charing Cross train. This view shows Cornwallis Bridge, built in 1885 at a cost of £10,000. It was a gift of Mr Frewin Stanley Wykeham (a member of the Cornwallis family), and has spans of 50 and 120 ft.

Locomotive No. 30924, 1957. This Schools class engine named *Haileybury* was built at Eastleigh in 1934. You can just make out the outline of a 6S class 201 Hastings DEMU (Diesel Electric Multiple Unit) at platform 1.

Locomotive No. 30929 at Cornwallis Villa, looking south from Braybrooke Terrace, 1957. The steam shows that the engine is active and ready to move. A valuable loco like this would never be left in a siding. The driver is having a cup of tea before shifting carriages which have been put out of the way of the main line before being taken to the sidings at Alexandra Park. It cannot possibly be a Charing Cross train, because it is facing the wrong way: a Schools class loco would not go to London in reverse!

Locomotive No. 30929 at Cornwallis Villa, looking east from Cornwallis Bridge, 1957. In this wonderful photograph the driver is eating his lunch on this class V Schools locomotive *Malvern*, built at Eastleigh in 1934. Pressure is up and the engine is ready to move. These sidings were removed in 1970, but the original Victorian signal box visible at the top right of the picture is still extant.

Locomotive 2MT, 1957. This British Rail standard small tank class 2MT, built 1956, is running round a train or just passing through. Little tank engines like this proved to be more economical and easier to service than larger engines, which often had to go to Ashford for repairs.

Q1 by gasworks, looking south from Braybrooke Road, 1957. Additional lightweight goods engines were needed on the Southern Railway during the Second World War, so every item not absolutely necessary was stripped away. This is why there are no running plates or wheel splashers. The Q1 proved an excellent 'war horse', which was able to pull trains of great length.

Locomotive No. 31406, looking north from Nelson Road, 1957. This beautiful class N Mogul (2–6–0) is venting steam while the driver waits for a signal to enter Hastings. These engines were used almost exclusively for passenger work until the Schools class was introduced. The end of a van on the extreme right of the picture reveals it is on goods duty.

Southern locomotive No. 828, looking north from Cornwallis Gardens, 1997. Local legend has it that the sandstone wall at Braybrooke Close was built by a family who intended to build a house, but the enormous wall cost so much to build that there was no money left for the house. The class S15 Maunsell SR 4–6–0, is a development of the Urie LSWR, built in 1927 at Eastleigh Works. It weighs 79 tons.

Goods yard, looking south from Earl Street Bridge, 1957. This view shows how busy the goods yard was before the decline of the railways. Note the now-demolished Railway Hotel and the roof of the ABC Cinema behind. You can also make out the Old Golden Cross and the turret of the Brassey Institute, both still extant. The engine in the foreground is an SECR L class 4–4–0 No. 31774, built at Ashford in 1914.

Locomotive No. 31498 at Raymond Hollands, 1957. This is the Wainwright class C 0–6–0 seen in the picture on p. 67 with the DEMU in front of the gasworks. Here, it is shunting some ex-SECR stock in the direction of the yard at Hastings station. The carriages are coupled in front of and behind the engine. Although this looks peculiar, it was quite common practice, and you can emulate it on your model railway.

Earl Street sidings, looking east from South Terrace, 1957. A passenger train is arriving from Rye and Ashford whilst a tank loco shifts some trucks. These small engines were very useful – they could operate forwards or backwards just as easily. St Mary's Terrace, where the first houses were built in 1827 by George Robinson, can be seen in the background.

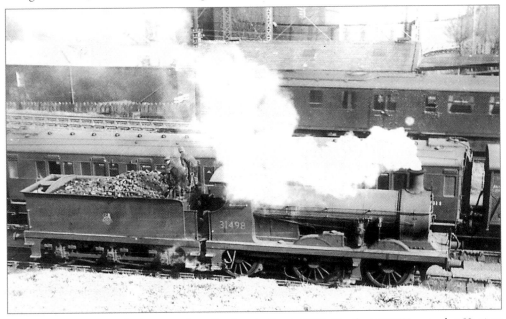

Locomotive No. 31498, looking east from Braybrooke Road, 1957. The first DEMU arrived at Hastings station on 23 February 1957. This is a particularly interesting photograph since in the foreground it shows two men coaling up a Wainwright class C 0–6–0 engine with a class 201 SR DEMU in the background. This very early DEMU was withdrawn because it emitted a squeal from the supercharger and people objected to it. Note also the SECR coach behind the locomotive.

Schools loco at Alexandra Park sidings, looking east from Braybrooke Road, 1957. The fireman is busy shovelling coal while the driver puts on steam to climb the gradient to Ore. There is old SECR stock in the sidings. The subway in the foreground is the one which goes to Waterworks Road from Lower Park Road.

THE CASTLE, WHITE ROCK & THE PIER

White Rock Baths, looking east, 1870. White Rock Place was formerly called Stratford Place, and before that Precursor Place. It was named White Rock on 7 October 1881. This view shows the brewery, demolished in 1885 when the Palace Hotel was built. The amazing urns have long since disappeared.

View of town centre, looking west from the castle, 1900. The wall on the right of the path may be part of the castle. The field where the Royal East Sussex Hospital was later built can be seen on the right-hand side of the picture.

Hastings Castle, looking west, 1910. This shows the remains of the collegiate church dissolved by Henry VIII in 1546, after which the site was abandoned. The castle was subsequently owned by the Pelham family from the seventeenth to the twentieth centuries. Hastings Corporation bought it in 1949. Do not confuse this castle with Duke William's Battle of Hastings campsite fort (the palisade with two towers depicted in the Bayeux Tapestry).

The new model village designed by Mr S. Deboo was opened on l9 February 1955. It featured buildings typical of the Sussex landscape. Oast-houses and timber-framed houses are visible in this picture. Vandalism which caused £5,000 worth of damage forced the village to close in 1972.

Floral clock, White Rock Gardens, 1937. The clock used to go 'Cuckoo, cuckoo, cuckoo' to denote the hours, but suffered a similar fate to the model village. The lettering on the clock gives the date away.

The pier, looking west, 1960. This view is from the Iron Age promontory fort known as the Ladies' Parlour. This fanciful name was coined when Hastings became a seaside resort. The damage to the hill in this picture was caused by an anti-aircraft gun emplacement during the Second World War.

Looking towards Caroline Place, 1930. Keep fit was a popular activity for visitors in the 1930s. The man on the left is using an early movie camera to record proceedings. Some of the houses on the parade behind were destroyed during the Second World War.

Caroline Place, looking west, 1910. You can just see a beach photographer at work beside the rowing boat in the centre. This was before the parade was widened.

Denmark Place, looking east, 1910. This was a popular part of the seafront near the Queen's Hotel. The pleasure yacht *The New Albertine* was a big attraction.

A coach arriving at Pelham Place, possibly with day visitors from London, 1963. The rebuilt Caroline Place is in the background.

Breeds Place, looking east, 1960. The bus is a Leyland Atlantean which replaced the trolley buses on 1 June 1959. A new network of routes was introduced with the new buses, and no. 151 (Ore to Hollington via Clive Vale) replaced the no. 11 trolley bus. The cars in the car park date from the late '30s: one of them is possibly a Riley. Both Mastin's famous draper's store and the attractive Breeds Place have now gone. This shows the reconstruction of the corner after the Second World War.

West Hill Lift, looking north, 1955. This is the top of the lift before the construction of the popular West Hill Café with its sea views.

West Hill Lift, 1905. Compare this with the previous picture. There is considerable erosion on the West Hill. Town events were often held here.

Caroline Place from Pelham Place, 1930. The top of the De Luxe Cinema is visible at the top right of the picture. Abraham's, the radio shop, used to be on the corner of Castle Street.

Breed's Place, 1960. This shows the Georgian terrace before demolition; Mastin's, a long-established local store, is also no more.

Pierrots on the beach at Carlisle Parade, looking west from near Harold Place, 1900. Pretty sunshades had not been invented at this time; instead the ladies protected their complexions with black umbrellas.

Carlisle Parade, looking east, 1920. The driver and the conductor are standing by the charabanc, a De Dion Bouton, registration number DY1436, in the hope of selling tickets to Bodiam Castle, Beachy Head or some such destination. The French car changed hands frequently, the first owner being Capt. W. Stewart in 1920, who used the trading name of *Purple Heather*. It was subsequently owned by the late Alderman Withers.

P. & A. Campbell's Britannia hovercraft is landing on the beach opposite Denmark Place, 23 May 1966. There is a large fan inside which blows downwards and makes a cushion of air on which the craft travels on land or on water. The propellers above give forward propulsion. It was very noisy, and seafront residents complained, until it broke down in the middle of the Channel. The passengers were rescued by the lifeboat.

The pier, 1963. This aerial view could be from before the war, but there is one thing that gives it away. Can you spot it?

White Rock, looking east, 1910. This appears to be a chilly day in autumn. The South Africa War Memorial was unveiled in 1903. It is made of pink granite and has flags made from gun metal. The jaunty lady in the background on the left is wearing an attractive outfit with fur-lined cuffs.

White Rock Place, looking north, 1880. This shows a late Victorian shop and restaurant at White Rock next to the Palace Hotel.

The Palace Hotel, looking north, 1887. This building replaced the early Victorian brewery at White Rock in 1885. The new Palace Hotel was opened on 7 August 1886.

White Rock Brewery, looking north, 1870. Built in 1831, it was demolished in 1885 when it was replaced by the Palace Hotel. Guinness's Dublin Stout remains popular.

White Rock Place, looking west, 1870. Walk along White Rock today, and you can discover nearly two hundred years of seaside architecture. Look for the bow-fronted Regency houses, ornate Victorian buildings and the 1920s White Rock Pavilion, now called a theatre. There is also a post-Second World War block of flats rebuilt on a bomb site.

Entrance to Robertson Street, 1939. The shop on the corner seems to change hands very frequently. Shop blinds are down, which makes this a summer scene. The man on the right is carrying a gas mask case, which dates the picture to the beginning of the Second World War.

White Rock, looking east, 1905. The man on the left has more interest in his newspaper than in the fashionable lady he is with. The deckchairs with canopies were a big attraction to lady visitors who were at great pains to protect their complexions from the sun: the paler your skin, the more of a lady you were.

White Rock Baths, looking west, 1905. Caves Oriental Café is across the road from the advertisement in this picture. You used to go in through a narrow shop which smelt of roasting coffee, behind which was a large restaurant. The decor was green and gold, with wicker chairs and glass topped tables. In the 1930s there was a trio of three lady musicians playing on a rostrum, one on a cello, another on a violin and the third on the piano.

White Rock Baths, looking east, 1900. The Palace Hotel has now been completed. The two men on the right of the picture appear to be wearing their hats the wrong way round, anticipating what many would regard as a more recent trend. The name Hallett (on the advertisement) appears in another picture in this book. Can you spot it?

Magdalen Swimming Bath For Ladies, looking west, 1902. This entrance led down to the small bath originally planned as an aquarium, but never completed as such. The small baths had green tiles which gave them a mysterious air. The large baths were finished in ice blue, and did not have so much charm.

White Rock Baths, looking west towards the pier, 1880. The Hastings and St Leonards Swimming Club was formed at the baths in 1888. Alderman Thorpe held the lease of the baths and Miss Knowles formed the Ducklings' Swimming Club for children in the 1920s.

White Rock Baths interior, 1932. Hastings Corporation took over the baths in 1925. Reconstruction and improvements took place, and the baths were re-opened on 27 June 1931. The bathers are wearing the regulation swimming costume of the period. The baths were the scene of numerous events – water polo, galas and swimming club fixtures.

Beach at White Rock, looking east, 1938. At first glance, the beachballs indicate that this is a post-war picture, but if you look closely you can see Lewcocks Restaurant (at Harold Place) and the Albany Hotel, which were destroyed during the war.

Bikers at the Yelton Hotel, 1990. Hastings has always been a popular destination for the motor-cycle fraternity. Yelton is the family name of the original owners, spelt backwards. Mr F.J. Notley was a hotelier, who started at No. 4. His daughter married Alderman Bouquet, who was a popular figure in Hastings.

The pier entrance, 1930. East Kent used to park their buses in Falaise Road between journeys, and this one is on its way back down to the seafront. The pavilion marked 'Dancing', at the far end of the pier, is the one built to replace the eastern-style structure which burnt down in 1917 (see p. 91).

The pier entrance, looking south, 1955. A quick glance at the zebra crossing dates this picture: they were first introduced into Hastings on 19 June 1954, and the last trolley bus ran on 30 May 1959, so it must be between these dates. Note that the pier has the Art Deco façade and minarets that are absent from the previous picture.

Triadome, looking south, 1966. This odd-looking structure was built to house the Hastings Embroidery, which consisted of twenty-seven panels of appliqué and embroidery work depicting the history of England between 1066 and 1966. It was subsequently used as an aquarium and then for pier amusements, before finally being removed.

Princess Alice, Countess of Athlone, accompanied by the Mayor, Councillor D.W. Wilshin, arriving at the Triadome to open the Hastings Embroidery, 25 May 1966. The man holding the umbrella is John Burton. The building behind, now demolished, was the Hastings Information Bureau.

The pier, looking north, 1989. This is the west side of the pier, showing the block of flats built on the site of the Grand Hotel. The Falaise Hall visible behind was designed by Sidney Little, the famous borough engineer known locally as the 'Concrete King' because he also designed the new seafront.

The pier entrance, looking south, 1895. The pier was opened on 9 August 1872 by Earl Granville, who described it as a 'peerless pier' – a title which perhaps it deserved if only for the handsome pavilion at the sea end, which was burned down in 1917. The pier was an immediate success – by 16 August that year it was attracting 4,000 people a day!

Queen Elizabeth opening the Triadome, 1966. It commemorated the 900th anniversary year of the Battle of Hastings.

The pier interior, looking north, 1980. The entrance to the Art Deco-style theatre, now used as a tea room, is on the right. The glass door has slanted panels which symbolise rays of light in the Art Deco style. The clock above was supplied by Dobell Bros, an old-established watchmaker and jeweller's in Robertson Street which traded for over a hundred years.

The pier ballroom, looking south, 1872. This is a close-up of the eastern-style pavilion which burned down in 1917. The picture shows that the landing stage was originally reached by way of this centre stairway.

The pier, looking south, 1900. The eastern-style pavilion was re-roofed and enlarged on 3 February 1899, and if you compare this with the previous picture you can see that it is different.

The pier entrance, looking south, 1905. The man with the pony and trap is hoping for business. He would take visitors out for a drive in the country, perhaps to Battle.

Pier head, looking south, 1905. This is such a pleasing picture that I could not resist including it. The steamer would go to Eastbourne, Rye Bay, or Boulogne and back. The pier subsequently lost the lucrative 'booze cruise' business to car ferries operating out of Folkestone and Dover.

White Rock Place, looking north from Hastings Pier, 1875. This shows the Victorian seafront before the sea wall was reconstructed. Some of the houses in this picture were destroyed by bombing. The houses above, in White Rock Road, are at an angle to the seafront, which is not apparent from the pier.

White Rock Gardens, looking east, 1935. The row of houses in White Rock Road are those which appear to be above the seafront in the previous picture. Look carefully and you can see they are the same.

The pier, 1920. The Grand Hotel on the left had friezes of tiles similar to the ones (now stolen) at the Buchanan Hospital, but it was badly built and fell into disrepair. The building on the right is the infirmary, which was demolished to make way for the White Rock Pavilion.

White Rock, 1935. Look closely at this photo, as it shows the derivation of the 'Oval' (where the fair goes in August) next to White Rock Gardens. The undamaged buildings on the seafront make this a pre-Second World War picture.

White Rock Pavilion, looking west, 1927. This shows the Spanish colonial-style building shortly after construction. The sign above refers to the 'municipal orchestra', which did not survive the war.

White Rock Pavilion, looking east, 1955. The two men on the roof are putting up a sign which reads 'Cyril Fletcher'. He was a comedian who lived in Sussex and was a great favourite with Hastings audiences. His famous catchphrase was 'Pin Back Your Lug 'oles!' This picture must be post-war, because of the zebra crossing.

Pier head, looking east, 1935. Before the Second World War, pleasure steamboat trips from the pier were a popular attraction. You can tell this picture dates from before the war because the Albany Hotel is still intact.

The pier entrance and the east end of Bottle Alley, 1958. The trolley buses are still running in this picture, so it is before 1959, but after 1954 when zebra crossings were introduced. The White Rock Pavilion is as it originally looked, before the addition of the terrace café.

Tea on the pier, looking north, 1950. This must have been an extraordinarily windless day for Hastings. There is not a hair out of place or a table cloth flapping in the breeze. The Grand Hotel behind is now derelict. It was found to have been very badly built.

The lights go on again: Eversfield Place from the pier, 1945. The war has just ended and it is August bank holiday. The pier was broken near the shore end to prevent the Germans from using it as a landing stage.

Angling is a popular sport in Hastings and here a father is trying to interest his son in the hobby, 1960.

ST LEONARDS

The London Road and Kings Road junction, looking north, 1907. The building on the right was originally opened as a Non-conformist British school on 23 November 1868. It comprised three school rooms built on the triangle of land between London Road and the then Gensing Station Road. This picture shows the original Christ Church, later the parish hall, with the school behind. The Congregational church, which has now lost its spire, can be seen in the distance.

Eversfield Place, looking west, 1905. A rough sea is always a source of fascination to visitors from inland who rarely experience the awesome power that the elements can deliver to the seafront on a windy day. Postcards of this subject were always popular, but bad weather severely damaged the sea wall and popular attractions like St Leonards Pier.

Eversfield Place, looking west, 1945. With the threat of invasion gone at the end of the war, people were allowed on to the seafront. Marine Court still shows bomb damage, and the forlorn remains of St Leonards Pier also bear witness to dark days. The dad in uniform has yet to be demobbed.

Eversfield Place, looking east, 1900. Named after a local land-owning family, this Victorian terrace was built before 1860 and would originally have been lodging houses. Before the increase in traffic, this was a popular area for small hotels. This view shows how the parade looked before the seafront was reconstructed.

Warrior Square and Queen Victoria's statue, looking north, 1903. Students from Hastings College once made a set of footprints from this statue to the Ladies and back, but this is not the only indignity the old Queen has suffered. She was machine-gunned in the war, and has a hole in her kneecap to prove it.

Warrior Square, looking west, 1920. The trams are still in operation, but the car (which looks like a Ford Model T) and the clothes show that we are entering the modern era.

Warrior Square Parade, looking east, 1935. The parade has been reconstructed, and the Victorian shelters are now sadly gone, but the fashions reveal this to be some fifteen years later than the previous picture.

Warrior Square Gardens, looking east, 1955. The bomb site on the other side of the square reveals this picture as post-war. The motor cars are another give-away, but the man with the handcart could belong to the last century.

Warrior Square from the end of Bottle Alley, looking west, 1960. You can tell this is after the war because of the missing buildings. It is also after 1959, since the trolley bus wires are gone. A rather unsightly public convenience has now been built here.

Grand Parade before Marine Court was built, looking west, 1899. The drinking fountain may be the one Robert Tressell remembered when he was writing *The Ragged Trousered Philanthropists*.

Grand Parade, looking east, 1935. The stone on the right marks the place where the St Leonards archway stood, forming the original entrance to Burton's St Leonards. Council workmen demolished it secretly in 1895. The work was done in the middle of the night to the fury of local residents, who woke up the next morning to find it gone. An interesting selection of vehicles enables us to date the picture. The shelters on the parade were demolished in the 1980s.

Elite Cinema fire, near Warrior Square, looking east, 1947. Opened in 1879 as an opera house, the cinema was bombed in the Second World War and re-opened in 1947, only to re-close immediately as a result of the fire. It is now a block of flats. The story is that the cinema caught fire at exactly midday, and the film to be shown was *Blaze at Noon*.

The pier, looking east, 1955. This is the lower part of Warrior Square. The picture is easy to date because of the zebra crossing.

London Road, looking north, 1906. All the trams were identical, except for those working the seafront. Trams which were not fitted with the Dolter stud-contact system had to reverse at the bottom of London Road. This tram connects to the electric overhead wires with a trolley pole, which you can see on the top deck. The dog is excitedly pulling the man upstairs for a ride to Silverhill.

London Road, looking north, 1890. This is the junction of London Road and Norman Road, showing the buildings which were destroyed during the Second World War. Only the two shops on the extreme left of the picture survived.

Grand Parade, looking east, 1930. The pier is without the minarets and still has the ballroom built in 1917. We can immediately date this picture to before the Second World War, as the buildings on the extreme left were bombed. On the parade you can see the 'sun traps' as they originally looked.

St Leonards Bank, 1899. This building is still in existence. You might enjoy going to look for it near Warrior Square.

House on fire in Dane Road, 15 April 1913. The St Leonards Fire Brigade, whose station was at Mercatoria, is in action in this picture. The house was owned by Henry Du Cros, the local MP, and had been fire-bombed by the Suffragettes. The house, called Levetleigh, was rebuilt as a most peculiar place, lacking a second storey.

Sheila Kaye-Smith, 1920. The famous novelist was born at Battle in 1887 and brought up in St Leonards. A doctor's daughter, she grew to love the local countryside, driving out with her father on his visits. Her books are a wonderful evocation of life in Sussex in the early twentieth century. They are also valuable for the now almost forgotten Sussex dialect. She was living opposite the house above when it burned down.

St Leonards Gardens, looking north, 1910. Gothic-style buildings were romantically built around the sides of this wooded valley. This was to contrast with the straight lines of the classical terraces on the seafront. The gardens had two ponds and a popular maze (which is the origin of the name Maze Hill), and deserve to be restored.

St Leonards Gardens, looking north, 1920. These gardens were laid out as a private garden for the Burton family. The town bought it for £9,000 in 1879; £2,000 of the money was raised by public subscription.

King's Library, Kings Road, looking west, 1901. Before the days of radio and television, newsagents like this were the prime source of the latest news. The boy and the girl are wearing black armbands to mourn the death of Victoria. Souvenirs of the late Queen hang above the doorway.

Gensing Gardens, St Leonards, looking north, 1897. These gardens were laid out in 1880. They were a warm and sheltered spot for sub-tropical plants.

The Colonnade, St Leonards Parade, looking west, 1875. This is the part of James Burton's 1830 Colonnade, which was destroyed to make way for Marine Court. The building nearest the camera was an hotel. Note the gas lamps. The Royal Victoria Hotel is just visible in the distance.

St Leonards Parade and pier, looking west, 1902. The elegance of old St Leonards is emphasised in this Edwardian view.

St Leonards Pier, looking south, 1895. The toll house on the right in this picture was demolished in a storm on 12 February 1899. The substructure of St Leonards Pier appears to be less strong than Hastings Pier, where the screws were set at an angle.

St Leonards Pier, looking north, 1899. Work started on St Leonards Pier in March 1888, and it was opened by Lord and Lady Brassey on 28 October 1891. The young man on the right is holding a pair of roller skates. The star spangled banner is flying and the band is playing. This picture shows the intricate ironwork of the pavilion at the shore end. The Royal Victoria Hotel is just visible on the extreme right of the picture.

Burton's St Leonards, looking east, 1900. This shows the classical Marina Terrace, now pulled down and replaced by Marine Court. To the right are the purpose-built shops designed by James Burton and opened in 1828.

St Leonards Pier from Marine Court, 1938. The new entrance looks like scenery from a film set. Notice the late Victorian ironwork of the pier below. The West Marina Esplanade was opened on 14 June 1878. The parade is 2,000 ft in length and is 50 ft wide. The sea wall is 15 ft thick.

St Leonards Pier, looking east, 1930. The old man on the left is taking a keen interest in the girls in their swimming costumes. The part of Burton's Colonnade that has now been replaced by Marine Court is in the background.

St Leonards Pier, looking north, 1930. This view is interesting because it shows areas of countryside which have now been developed. Also visible in the distance are the seventeen arches of the now sadly demolished viaduct on the Sidley to Crowhurst railway line.

Roller hockey on St Leonards Pier, 1934. This was an exciting sport on roller skates. This view shows the interior of the building marked 'rink', on the end of the pier on the aerial photograph on p. 115.

Marine Hotel, looking west, 1929. Local historian Barry Funnell used to say that there were cabbages growing in the flower bed behind the railings. This photograph shows the hotel to be in a poor state of repair, underlining the financial situation of the proprietors. The foundation stone for Marine Court was laid on 30 November 1936 by the Chairman of the Southern Railway, R. Holland-Martin.

St Leonards Pier, 1930. Here we can see the influence of American films, as this is an attempt to create a modern style totally incongruous with the Victorian pier — but a reminder of the popular cinemas of the period.

Marine Court, looking north, 1948. Built to look like an ocean liner, this was the tallest block of flats in the country. In May 1937 a £5 contest to name Marine Court also came up with 'Sunny South Court', 'Monstrosity Mansions', 'Have No Care House', 'Mammon Court', and 'Controversy Building'. Bomb damage is shown in this photo.

Royal Victoria Hotel, looking north, 1938. This hotel was built in 1828 by James Burton, and enlarged in 1903. If you put one hand over the attic and top storey and the other over the porch, you can see what the building originally looked like.

A girl with her parents on St Leonards beach, 1938. The little girl is wearing a ruched swimming costume. It was made with elastic and the idea was that it would grow with the child. She is holding a wooden spade and fork with which to build a sandcastle. Beach photography became more practical as a commercial trade with the introduction of the roll film camera, invented by Kodak.

St Leonards Steam Fire Brigade, 1861. The local fire brigade was formed in 1861, and there were three sections. Sections 1 and 2 were at Hastings, and 3 was based at Mercatoria in St Leonards. They later moved to Shepherd Street. Each section consisted of thirteen men, a superintendent, a surgeon and a secretary. There were nearly seventy volunteers for these thirty-nine places. The steam engine in the picture cost £80, and the volunteers practised early in the morning.

St Leonards Pier, looking north, 1910. Older people will remember that name-punching machines like this survived on Hastings Pier until the 1960s. The little girl beside her father is wearing a beautifully trimmed hat, so this is a holiday occasion.

Windmill Road, near Silverhill junction, looking west, 1901. The original Silverhill Mill, known as Drapers Mill, was destroyed by fire in 1865. This mill was rebuilt for Drapers in 1866 by the Upfield firm, who were agricultural engineers at Catsfield. It was worked until 1941, after which the structure was left to rot. Final plans for demolition were passed in 1966.

Baldslow Mill, 1900. This mill lost its sails in 1900 and worked by steam until 1930, when it was converted into a private house. The name Baldslow is said to come from Beald's Hill; it is spelled 'Baldeslei' in the Domesday Book. The site was used for one of the beacons which were lit when the Spanish Armada sailed up the Channel in 1588.

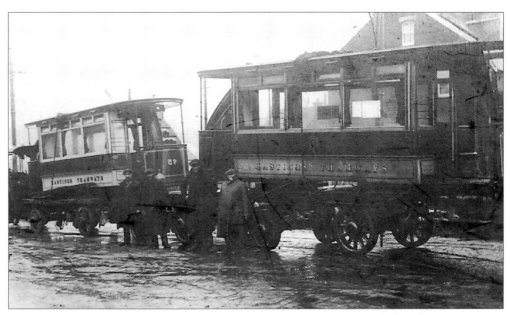

Trams being removed to Maidstone, 1914. This may be Beaufort Road. The trams are being taken from Hastings to Tilling-Stevens, where they were to be converted from the electric Dolter stud-contact system to petrol-driven engines. They were subsequently re-converted to electricity (trolley pole method) in 1921.

Lady tram conductor, 1917. The First World War heralded changing roles for women in British society. Hastings Tramway's first lady conductor started in 1916. She earned less than a man. The basic rate for a tram conductor was 4*d* an hour for a sixty hour week, which made £1. A driver got 6*d* an hour, top rate, for sixty hours.

Bathing pool, looking south, 1935. The bathing pool was opened in 1933, and was a great success – it admitted 33,000 in June of that year. It was a fashionable place, and parades like this were held. Modern bathing suits were daring to those who could remember the 'good old days'.

Wishing Tree, looking north near Gillsman's Hill, 1900. The signpost is marked Hollington and Crowhurst in one direction, and Bexhill in the other. Long ago, a lady from Bexhill claimed that her grandfather, Robert Deudney, named a tree 'Wishing Tree' while playing a game with his children. In 1961 an oak tree was planted in the middle of the roundabout at Gillsman's Hill to replace the original Wishing Tree felled in the scheme.

Outside the bathing pool, looking east, 1931. The charm of the bathing pool was that you could alternate between swimming in the pool and going outside into the sea. Organised games were popular on the terrace.

Beating the bounds, Hollington, 1910. The boy is being held upside down in a bumping ceremony which dates from the time before there were accurate maps. The older inhabitants would make the local boys remember where the parish boundaries were by banging their heads against the boundary stone. A less painful alternative was to use sticks, hence the expression 'beating the bounds'. The first really accurate maps to show parish boundaries were the tithe maps, drawn in about 1840.

Filsham Road, looking west, 1900. The foreground shows the Hastings to Charing Cross railway line and the South Saxons playing fields. The coastline leading to Bexhill can be seen in the distance.

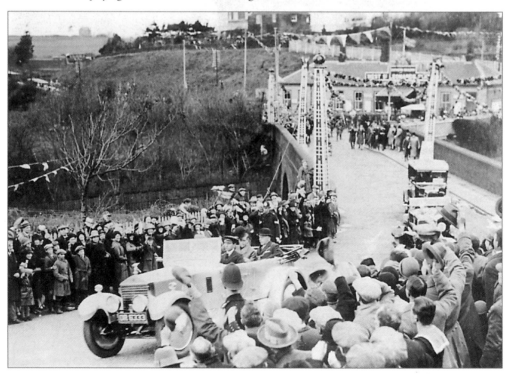

West St Leonards station, 1927. The Prince of Wales, later Edward VIII, arrived at West St Leonards station on 6 April 1927 and was met by the Mayor, T.H. Dymond. He spent the entire day in Hastings, and was observed to become very bored.

Terrier tank No. 32636, looking east from West Marina station, 1957. This A1X 0–6–0 Terrier tank used to bring the circus train to Hastings. It normally worked on the Kent & East Sussex Railway, and is down at West Marina to have the tubes cleaned as part of a general 'wash and brush up'. It is doing a bit of light duty taking trucks to the coaling station. This particular engine has been preserved on the Bluebell Railway.

ACKNOWLEDGEMENTS

I should like to thank Hastings Museum & Art Gallery for permission to use photos. Thanks to Victoria Williams, curator, and Cathy Walling, assistant curator.

Thanks are also due to the following:

Alan Mitchell of the Sheila Kaye-Smith Society for the picture of Sheila Kaye-Smith; J. Manwaring Baines for the use of his original slides and historical information; Ron Fellows for historical information and the use of his postcard collection; Pamela Haines for the fashion and architecture captions; Pauline Crouch for helping me with the Introduction and the Circus Parade captions; Polly O'Keefe for the Flower Seller caption; John Powys for identifying old cars and allowing me to make prints from his irreplaceable negatives of steam trains taken in the 1950s; David Padgham for the use of his postcards and providing historical information about buses and trams; Jane of Photo Express, Kings Road, St Leonards, for providing technical advice and contact papers; Supersnaps of Queen's Road for making prints from slides; Mr Maxwell of Salmons Bookshop for rescuing the Lazarus glass plates; Brian Green of the Fisherman's Museum for information about the luggers.

Lastly, we should not forget the late Barry Funnell whose spirit lives on in the pages of this book.

Hastings Carnival Queen, 1966. Beehive hairstyles were popular when this photo was taken of the Carnival Queen and her attendants. The bus in the background is a Leyland Atlantean.

BRITAIN IN OLD PHOTOGRAPHS

To order any of these titles please telephone our distributor, Littlehampton Book Services on 01903 721596
For a catalogue of these and our other titles please ring Regina Schinner on 01453 731114